"My friend Ron Owens, with the heart of a musician, has researched and authored the modern version of the hero-martyrs of Hebrews 11:35-40. It is the stirring record of what it means to be a 'real' Christian. It is my prayer that those who read this book will join God's orchestra and at the cost of death itself—keep the music going to His praise and glory." —Stephen F. Olford, Founder and President, Olford Ministries International, Memphis, TN

"This is a story of love and devotion to God and family. It is impossible to conceive how a person's faith could blossom in the midst of the spiritual wasteland during that time in Russia's history. This is the testimony of God's grace as well as a confrontation to our easy lifestyle." —John Sullivan, Executive Director, Southern Baptist Convention of Florida

"This is a startling challenge to all believers, and a shocking rebuke to North American ease-loving Christians claiming to be followers of Christ. I encourage every believer to read this book. It will be hard to read without tears. In a day when real heros are few, parents would do well to read this to their children, and young people will be challenged to make an investment of their lives to God and His glory." —Ralph Sutera, Canadian Revival Fellowship

"Please don't speed-read this book. Read it meditatively. See and feel the events surrounding Georgy's life, and then let the lessons from his life sink into your heart. You will never be the same again. Then go out and share this book with somebody else. They will thank you." —Warren Wiersbe, Author and Conference Speaker

"This story of Georgy Slesarev's martyrdom will live with you forever. Your perspective of witnessing will never be the same again. It is strikingly appropriate in today's increasing climate of discrimination and persecution. This is a worthy addition to *Fox's Book of Martyrs.*" —Avery Willis, International Mission Board, Southern Baptist Convention

...they could not stop the music.

...they could not stop the music.

The Life and Witness of Georgy Slesarev

First Violinist, Bolshoi Theater Orchestra, Moscow

By Ron Owens

Fresh Springs Publications
Kingsport, Tennessee

Editing and layout design by Jan McMurray

THEY COULD NOT STOP THE MUSIC

ISBN 1-886797-06-4

Printed in the United States of America.

To Anna Georgiyevna Davydova (little Anna),

who first asked me the question,

"Have you heard about my father?";

and to the memory of her parents, Anna and Georgy.

CONTENTS

x

PROLOGUE

When 74-year-old Moscow voice teacher Anna Georgiyevna Davydova asked me if I had heard of her father, little did I realize that I was about to embark on a two year journey with a man who would deeply impact my life. Nor could I have imagined that the journey would lead me to a new understanding of what the cross can mean in the life of a Christian who believes that Jesus was speaking directly to him when He said: *"You shall be witnesses to Me in Jerusalem, and in all Judea and Samaria, and to the end of the earth"* (Acts 1:8). The story you are about to read personifies what Jesus was saying to His disciples when He used the word *witness*. The Greek word for *witness* is "martus," from which we get the English word "martyr." For most of those disciples, the cost of being the Lord's *witness* would be martyrdom. In deciding to be *"witnesses of these things"* (Luke 24:48), they were choosing to accept what Jesus had said when He first commissioned them to go. He had explained what it would cost them to follow Him: *"If anyone desires to come after Me, let him deny himself, and take up his cross daily, and follow Me. For whoever desires to save his life will lose it, but whoever loses his life for My sake will save it"* (Luke 9:23-24).

When I began writing this story I thought it would be about a Christian musician and the suffering and ultimate martyrdom he endured in a Siberian gulag. But the more I interviewed and read, the more I realized that the real story of Georgy[1] Georgiyevich Slesarev's life was not his suffering and martyrdom, it was his *witness*. And I became convinced that this would be the story he would want told. [2]

I had not been writing long before I also discovered that the writing of a biography is like the assignment given to spring: to bring to life again. It is the attempt to recover the heartbeat of someone whose life has already been lived, and the more I discovered of Georgy's life, the greater the challenge was to pass on the spirit and passion of this man who deliberately *chose* the cross over the easier path so many of us might have taken. The easier path would have been not to tell anyone about

---

1 Pronounced Gay-or-ghee

2 After the fall of the *Iron Curtain* there was a period of time when relatives of those victimized by the Stalin purges were able to visit the KGB headquarters to read and photocopy the official records kept of their loved ones from their arrest to their release, or death. Much of the information in this story was obtained from these files by Georgy's daughter, who was nine years old at the time of the arrest. Among the material she found on file was an account in her father's own handwriting of his life up until the night of his arrest. He was ordered to write this account by his interrogators, and from his attention to detail, it is obvious that he gladly complied, hoping the document would serve as a witness to anyone who would read it. The personal quotes and detailed recollection of family history, his conversion and his witnessing all come directly from this handwritten document. In addition to the written records she photocopied, they gave her the actual file photos of her father. She was also granted permission to copy some additional information by longhand, such as the names of the choir members who also were arrested the night of January 21, 1935. Other information in this story comes from firsthand written accounts of those whose lives Georgy touched, both before his arrest and during the rest of his life in the communist "slave-labor" camps.

his faith, especially knowing that with each *witness* the persecution would increase. In writing this story I have been forced to look inward and ask myself the question, "What would I do if faced with such a choice?" Hopefully I would pass the test, but then, Peter was convinced that he would. Peter's denial of his Lord was actually his refusal to be a *witness*. And he refused because of fear. Georgy's courageous choice to be a *witness* was what ultimately led to his being *martyred*.

Unlike Georgy, most of us will never be called on to make decisions that will determine whether we will physically live or die. Like Georgy, however, we *are* called on daily to decide whether or not we will be *witnesses*. The choices we make reflect what is most important to us. The little choices reveal what is in our heart.

A. W. Tozer said: *"The heart that learns to die with Christ soon knows the blessed experience of rising with Him, and all the world's persecutions cannot still the high note of joy that springs up in the soul that has become the dwelling place of the Holy Spirit."*[8] This describes Georgy Georgiyevich Slesarev. Because of the unquenchable joy in his heart, nothing could silence his *witness*. Try as they would, **they could not stop the music.**

---

3 "The Old and the New Cross" (pamphlet) Christian Publications, Camp Hill, PA

ACKNOWLEDGMENTS

Special thanks to:

—Fresh Springs Foundation of Kingsport, Tennessee, for publishing this book

—Henry Blackaby Ministries for partnering with us in servicing and distributing of the Slesarev story

—Anna Georgiyevich Davidova, who has been such a resource, encouragement and inspiration

—Alexander, Timofey and Kirill, the interpreters and translators without whom the book could not have been written

—Evgeny Goncharenko, director of the Logos Choir, Orchestra, and Music Academy, for continuing the ministry of Georgy Slesarev through the arts.

—all those who committed themselves to praying for me during the two years of research and writing

—all those who were willing to take the time to read and to write their encouraging comments on the manuscript

—our God, the God of Georgy Georgyevich Slesarev, who has never failed to keep His promises to never leave us nor forsake us

Prelude #1

"BIG"

The Bolshoi Theater is the home of the world famous Bolshoi Ballet which was established in 1825, just after the building was completed. It became renowned for its elaborately staged productions of the classics and of children's ballet that preserved the traditions of the nineteenth century classical dance. Originally built between 1821 and 1824, the theater was rebuilt in 1856 after a fire. Its exterior architecture, with its eight giant white columns and four great horses rearing in the traces of Apollo's chariot above them, is a magnificent sight to behold. Its elegant five-tiered interior, furnished in gilt and red velvet, seats more than 2000 people.

The Bolshoi Theater

In the Russian language the word Bolshoi means "big" or "great," and it is definitely "greatness" that the Bolshoi has stood for in the world of the theater over the years. In addition to housing the Bolshoi Ballet, the theater is also the home of the Bolshoi Opera, where in 1922 the premiere of Tchaikovsky's *Eugene Onegin* was acclaimed as a major reform in opera. It was about that time that Georgy Slesarev began playing in the Bolshoi Theater Orchestra.

One

JANUARY 21, 1935
10:30 p.m.

Snow was falling lightly as Georgy Georgiyevich Slesarev closed the Petrovka Street stage door behind him. He had just finished a performance of *Khovanshchina*, Moussoursky's opera about the political and religious strife taking place in Russia in 1682 at the time Peter The Great was coming to power. As a musician, Georgy was very grateful for the experience of playing his violin in such a prestigious orchestra, but strange as it may seem, he found his greatest fulfillment in talking, or as he called it, *witnessing*, to people during the intermissions. "It is always easy to engage someone in conversation," he'd say, "especially when they recognize me as being one of the performers." He was almost always able to take something from whatever opera or ballet was being performed and apply it to life and the need to know God. He was convinced that God had opened the door to the Bolshoi so that he could be His *witness* there.

He paused for a moment to take a deep breath. The lights from Moscow's Central Department Store across the street provided a perfect backdrop for the large glistening snowflakes that seemed in no hurry to reach the ground. As he turned to walk down Petrovka street, he was already anticipating the warmth of the two small rooms where he and his wife Anna Gorlova Vasilyevna lived with their two small children, "little Anna" and Mikhail. "God has been

3

so good to me," he thought to himself, as he carefully nestled his violin under his arm and began the twenty minute walk home. These walks had become very special to him. Often he would spend the entire time praying, and always, unless it was too cold or raining, he would take off his hat to pray. Down Neglinaya Street, through Trubnyaya Square, walked Georgy, praying. He would pray for his family. He would pray for those he was *witnessing* to.

young Georgy

He would pray for his church and for the instrumental ensemble he directed. He would pray for the strength to keep pressing on in spite of the increased governmental persecution of Believers. Past the Sandunovski Bath

House where he, Anna, and the children went every Saturday for their bath. Visiting the Bath House had become one of the weekly highlights for the children, an adventure that would begin with a ride in a horse and carriage or, at this time of year, a horse and sleigh with, of course, the bells. They loved the bells.

Tonight, however, his mind began to wander back to his own childhood days growing up in Stoderevskaya, in the Mozdokskoi district of the Caucasus mountains. Who would have ever guessed what God had in store for him? At an early age Georgy's parents and teachers had observed his unusual musical gifts. He had inherited his Kubansky Cossack father's fire and talent, and under some of the finest training he had developed into an outstanding violinist. Now, though only 32, he had been playing first violin in the prestigious Bolshoi Theater Orchestra for nine years.

It had been an interesting journey. Georgy's father had come from a poor Cossack family. At the age of 18 he had decided to join the Tersky Troops to serve out his obligatory military service. It was during this time that he learned to play the trumpet. His natural talent and hard work soon earned him a position in the military band as well as a place in the Tersky choir where, for the first time, he came into contact with Christians. He was so amazed and impressed at their high moral standards and behavior that he began trying to emulate them in everything he did.

At 29 Georgy's father married into a very strict patriarchal Orthodox family, and in the beginning of the marriage regularly attended the Orthodox church with his wife. Then when Georgy was 6 years old the family moved farther east, where providentially (and Georgy was convinced it was God's providence), his father was reunited with a younger brother who was now a Baptist minister. It had been many years since they had had any contact, and it was at this point his father felt he heard and understood the message of the gospel for the first time. He soon became a Believer.

Here, sad to say, was the beginning of a rift between Georgy's father and mother over their respective interpretations of what it meant to be a Christian. As time went by the tension over his having been what he called "born again" became more and more serious. In his newfound zeal for God he tried to convert his wife and in the process unwisely began to criticize the Orthodox Church. His criticism only led to greater alienation and many arguments. In an effort to avoid as much conflict as possible he decided to stop attending any Baptist meetings, except on rare occasions. But this decision did not help. His wife's relatives began telling the five children horrible stories about Baptists. In their ignorance of who Baptists were they accused them of being controlled by Satan. Some even said that Baptists sacrificed their children and ate them, though they themselves had never been to a Baptist meeting.

Georgy remembered how God's grace began to express itself through his father and how little by little his father had changed. He became increasingly compassionate toward those who were attacking him, and though he would have rather attended the Baptist church, he would go with the family every Sunday to the Orthodox Temple. At every opportunity, however, he encouraged the children to read the Bible and when he could, he would teach them the Scriptures. His favorite Bible passage was Psalm 15.

"LORD, who may abide in Your tabernacle? Who may dwell in Your holy hill? He who walks uprightly, and works righteousness, and speaks the truth in his heart; He who does not backbite with his tongue, nor does evil to his neighbor, nor does he take up a reproach against his friend...."

Georgy remembered how his father encouraged the children to do everything they could to keep peace in the family, even as he himself strove to hold the family together. But being just a child Georgy didn't understand a lot of what was going on, and he continued to be dominated by a fear of Baptists, a fear that was continuously being reenforced by his mother.

Then one day he and his father happened to be together in Petygorsk in the north Caucusus. They saw a Baptist church and decided to attend a meeting. That night Georgy's fear of Baptists was immediately dispelled, and his heart began to open to the Lord. He realized that Baptists were ordinary, simple people, who just loved God and wanted to serve Him. Their buildings were different, as was their form of worship, but that didn't seem to bother him now.

It was about this time that something else happened that greatly impacted his life. Shortly after the family had moved to Vladykaskaz a very special person arrived in town. He was an Orthodox Church monk, and through his total commitment to Christ and the sermons he preached, he began inspiring the whole town. Georgy's soul was ignited, and he began to attend all the services and listen to everything this man said. He became so inspired that at one point he even considered becoming a monk himself.

Though only 13 he was already finishing Music Academy. His father, however, did not want him to study music because he himself had experienced how thorny the road of a musician could be. What he really desired was that his son enter the "noble and honest" profession of school teaching. But from childhood Georgy had developed a passion for the violin, so he begged his father to allow him to pursue violin studies. His father surrendered to his pleas but did not change his mind about what he wished his son to become.

Georgy's father

Now as he walked past the Sandunovski Bath House, Georgy recalled how the tension in the home had begun to get worse. Friends of his mother had encouraged her to file for divorce. His father hadn't known what to do. In a desperate move he decided to ask Father Fadey, the monk, to intervene. The night Father Fadey visited their home, Georgy's father was away, which, as Georgy remembered, was again the providence of God. Father Fadey reminded his mother of the vows she had made under God to her husband and told her she must not divorce. He then talked about Georgy's having been given a talent that he must not bury but must diligently develop for God's glory. He said Georgy should forget about the monastery or teaching school.

After hearing what Father Fadey had said, Georgy's father had begun taking him to play violin in various summer-season orchestras. On one of those occasions they attended another Baptist meeting, where for the second time Georgy felt the sweet warmth of fellowship of the Baptist Believers. He soon turned his life over to God. "I felt that everyone was next of kin to me," he remembered thinking. "I felt a very special love for God's children. I was touched to the depths of my soul by a Scripture text that hung on the wall of that little church: *The blood of Christ cleanses us from all sin.*"

From this point on his life had become a kaleidoscope of events, with further education at the Technical College of Krasnodr in the North Caucasus, singing lessons, military service playing in military orchestras and violin concert tours. He had been enjoying much success with the public as well as receiving very positive reviews from critics when, in 1923, just six years after the Bolshevic Revolution, he found himself in

Moscow. Could it really be twelve years ago? he thought, as he walked across Trubnyava Square. Twelve years since he first began attending services at the 2nd Congregation of Baptists in Moscow, where soon, a growing desire to move closer to the Lord led him to be baptized into the membership of the church.

He smiled to himself as he thought of the letter he had written to his father about the baptism. Because of the family conflict his father had never made that step, but the letter so impacted him that though it was in the dead of winter and a hole had to be cut in the ice, he decided to be baptized immediately. This decision proved to be too much for his wife, and he was driven from his home.

These thoughts, as well as the fulfillment he was now experiencing through his ministry at the church, were flooding Georgy's mind and soul as he approached his apartment complex, a building that stood between Sergievsky and Bolshoesergievske Lanes. Tonight he would go in the #20 Sergievsky Lane entrance. If he had entered through the Bolshoeserievske door he would have noticed a black sedan parked 50 meters away. He would have recognized it as one of the many "Black Marias" used by the GPU, the Soviet Secret Police.[1] In recent months there had been rumors of a new wave of arrests, arrests almost always made under cover of darkness to keep this hideous government activity hidden from neighbors as much as possible. He had no idea what was about to unfold that night as he climbed the steps. All he knew was that Anna would be waiting for him.

---

1 GPU stood for State Political System and was used from 1922 until 1946 when it was changed to MGB, initials for Soviet secret police. In 1953 it was again changed to KGB, an acronym for State Security Committee

Interlude #1

THE ARREST

Most arrests were made at night. Resistance was considered to be futile; at least, that's how people felt. Though innocent of the charges, few ever made a scene. Seldom did anyone cry out in protest or try to escape. But what if citizens had resisted? What would have happened when a quarter of Leningrad was arrested? What if the secret police knew that every time they knocked on a door their own lives would be in danger? Would things have been different? But it just wasn't done. Being arrested was considered to be a part of fate.

Two

11:45 p.m.

They shared the four room apartment with three other family units; a family of three, plus two couples. Because Georgy and Anna had two children they were blessed to have been given two of the four rooms. One room was a bedroom which the four of them used, and the other served as a kitchen and living area. There was no gas or electricity so Anna did all her cooking on a small kerosene stove. The apartment was heated by hot water provided by the city. That was how the whole city got its heat and hot tap water. At this time of night, however, the heat was already turned off, so the bowl of hot borscht Anna had prepared was most welcome, as would be the blankets they would soon be sharing.

By now it was almost midnight. The children were sound asleep. As Georgy and Anna rose from the table to thank God for His provision, they were startled by someone pounding on the door. The immediate sensation in the pits of their stomachs was the feeling millions of others have experienced over the years, whether Huguenots in France, Jews in Nazi Germany, or fellow Russian citizens. With the instant knot in the stomach comes the flush of fear that envelopes the entire body. Fear that it is their turn; fear that they are next. Several church members had been arrested some time before, and among them was fellow Christian musician, Yakov Vyzovsky, who just disappeared into the night never to be

13

heard of again. Three choirs had also been arrested that night. But that was nine years ago, about the time Georgy had begun playing with the Bolshoi Theater orchestra.

The pounding on the door grew louder. What if they didn't answer? It would give him and Anna at least a little more time together. But he knew it would do no good to resist. He pulled the latch and opened the door. Three men in secret police uniforms pushed their way into the room. One of them, holding the arrest warrant, said: "You are Georgy Giorgiyevich Slesarev?"

"Why?" Georgy asked.

"You have been operating as a counter-revolutionary," came the reply, "and, according to Article 58 of the criminal code, you have been declared an enemy of the State." Article 58.[1] An enemy of the State! Georgy and Anna had just recently heard of Article 58. It was now being used in the arrest of so-called "offenders" since the murder of Kirov,[2] just 51 days before.

---

1 #58 was the most often used article of the communist criminal code. It had 14 sub-points that covered any excuse to arrest a citizen. It was under this article that most Christians were apprehended.

2 Sergei Mironovich Kirov was the Leningrad communist boss. He was one of Stalin's closest friends and frequent companion. Kirov was an exceptionally popular politician with unusual warmth and charisma. In spite of this "warmth," Kirov alone was responsible for, as Aleksandr Solzhenitsyn described it, the washing of millions of men and women down the "gulag sewers" of Siberia, their only crime being counted among those "insects" to be used as slave labor in the work-camps of Siberia. Kirov was murdered on December 1, 1934. A young man, Leonid Nilolayev was arrested and immediately executed. The Party catapulted Kirov into martyrdom. It has since been discovered, however, that Stalin, needing a excuse to launch his first wave of arrests, actually had his "friend" Kirov murdered.

14

Before they could protest, the secret police pushed them aside and began the search of their two rooms. Nothing was sacred. Closets were emptied. Every drawer had its contents dumped on the floor. Beds were overturned, and mattresses ripped open. By now little Anna and Mikhail were clinging to their parents as they watched things precious to them being trampled beneath dirty wet boots. They pulled Georgy's books off the shelves and threw them to the floor, after looking through each one for evidence. Though he was in no way wealthy, Georgy had been able to amass an enviable library.

Unknown to Georgy, the authorities had already intercepted letters he had written to Christians outside the country, several in Germany and two in the United States. In 1932 he had taught violin to a German Baptist student who was in Russia learning the language. When the student had returned to his home they had exchanged several letters and postcards. These had been intercepted and read and copies of them were added to a file they were preparing on Georgy. Some of the content was of a Christian nature and considered to be anti-government. This was used to claim that Georgy had ties to counter-revolutionary organizations in the West. They were now looking for further evidence of this kind, as well as anything else that might be considered subversive.

Suddenly one of the GPU agents beckoned to his comrades. They had found some addresses, and they had found the little box containing the letters that Georgy had written to Anna during their courtship, letters that revealed his longing to have a "Christ-filled home" in the middle of an atheistic world. These letters and addresses would be all the evidence needed to convict him, not that evidence was needed. Everyone knew that once the arrest procedure had begun there was no turning back. Evidence could always be fabricated. And there was always someone, a neighbor, a witness, who would bring accusations against the arrested party. The trials were shams. In any case, Article 58 covered every contingency.

As Georgy watched, he realized how desperately Anna and the children needed what no human could provide. At that moment he knew their only refuge was in the Lord. He began to silently pray. "O God, help them. You're the only One who is going to be able to." The fear and foreboding that had been playing games with his emotions began to be replaced by the miraculous gift of Gods' peace. "If God is who He says He is, then He knows what is happening," he thought. "There can be no time when things get out of control for Him. Surely He knows what is going on right now in this apartment. God is watching them read the letters. God knows what is going to happen."

The search finally ended and the GPU agents gathered up their "evidence." They motioned for Georgy to follow them. At that moment, Anna, who had outwardly been able to keep her poise for the sake of the children, suddenly cried out, "But how are we going to live without you? Where will we get money to eat? Where are we going to live?" This sudden outburst startled the agents. They paused. Georgy walked to the window, pulled back the curtain and looked out into the darkness. The snow was still falling. What could he say? His mind was racing. Would he ever see his family again? Would this be the last time they'd be together? Would he ever know what happened to them? *"Boże pomogy! Boże pomogy!"* he prayed. "God help! God help!"

With his back still towards them, Anna heard her husband say words to which she would cling, words she would never forget, words that were to prove true through the years of adversity yet to come, *"If God has allowed this to happen there will not pass one day when your needs will not be met. We must trust Him."*[3]

---

3 Several times during the days Anna Georgiyevna Davydova, Georgy's daughter, was being interviewed by the author, she mentioned those final moments in the apartment with her father. What he said left an indelible imprint on her young heart. She gave testimony to the absolute faithfulness of God during the years that would follow. There never was a day when their needs were not met.

Family picture of Georgy, Anna, and little Anna

Interlude #2

LUBYANKA

Lubyanka was, and still is, the popular designation for the building where the Secret Police headquarters was housed. Lubyanka derived its name from an adjoining street and square. Before the Revolution of 1917, the building had housed the Rossiya Insurance Company. It is still the headquarters of the KGB. Here the arrested were interrogated, sentenced, and detained for a brief period before being moved to another Moscow prison prior to being shipped to Siberia. Many of those arrested, and who were eventually released, testified that after the time spent in the prisons of Moscow, even the work-camps of Siberia seemed a relief. To this day the mention of Lubyanka is a reminder to the Russian people of a part of their history that, in its atrocities and ignominy, is unparalleled in the chronicles of nations. Nowhere on earth has human life been considered to be as inconsequential as within the walls of Lubyanka.

Three

JANUARY 22
12:50 a.m.

Escorted by the two GPU agents, Georgy left his apartment. The snow had stopped falling. It was colder. Emotions he was feeling for the first time in his life engulfed him. Those for whom he would have laid down his life at a moment's notice were being left behind. Would he ever see them again? How was Anna going to explain what had happened to the children? Would he, like his friend Yakov Vyzovsky, just disappear? Was there no one who could help? How could this be happening? He had done nothing wrong. How could they say he was an enemy of the people?

They reached the car, and as two of the agents threw the "evidence" in the trunk, the other pushed Georgy into the back seat. He tried to catch a last look at the door that he, Anna, and the children had so often walked through, but the windows of the "Black Maria" were covered with frost.

What would his fellow members in the orchestra say when he didn't show up at rehearsal? Probably very little. A new member of the first violin section would be introduced and would sit in Georgy's chair. Nobody would ask what happened. The word might be whispered among a few, but they wouldn't say anything. It was safer not to talk. Eyes would ask the questions and eyes would reply. Or perhaps a slight nod would say all that was needed.

Georgy, the Christian *witness*, had been arrested. Everyone just knew.

What was going to happen to the choir and musicians back at church? How would they react? He knew. They would do as they had always done in such situations, incidents that were now becoming increasingly frequent. They would pray for him. Nothing else could be done. But was that not the most important thing they could do? This would prove to be so true in the hours and days ahead. Would he ever play a violin again? It had been a part of his life for as long as he could remember.

Lubyanka, Headquarters of the Secret Police

He didn't have to ask where they were going. He knew. Lubyanka. He had heard the rumors. Now he was about to find out first hand how true they were. He thought of trying to melt the frost on the window with his hand but realized how useless that would be. What good would it do to know where they were driving? Then they were there. Well, almost. He heard the agents swearing among themselves about the Lubyanka congestion. There were so many Black Marias arriving from their ignominious assignments that it was impossible to find a place to park near the building. Two of the agents were going to have to walk Georgy up the street while the other waited in the car. If they were going to make the third arrest assigned to them that night, they would have to get Georgy checked in quickly.

Interlude #3

THE PROCESS

From the moment you were selected for arrest, your fate was predetermined. There was no defense or proof of innocence that would change the minds of those standing in judgment. All that was left was a mock trial and the handing out of the sentence that, for most, would lead to oblivion. The procedure did not take long. Before you realized what was really happening, your sentence had been read, you had been fingerprinted, photographed, and thrown in a cell. It had to be a dream. You would wake up. A mistake had been made. Somehow you would be able to reason with them . . . .

KGB file photo of Georgy

Four

THE BEGINNING OF THE
REST OF YOUR LIFE

As he was led into the hallway there was a line of
what seemed to be 20 or more people waiting to be
"checked in." The despair on their faces told it all. Each
would have his own personal story to tell of that night,
that is, if any of them were ever given the opportunity. He
was surprised to see several women in the line, then
shocked, when he found himself looking into the eyes of
Sister Shalier, a member of the church choir. What was she
doing here? Why had she been arrested? How he wished
he could stop to encourage her, but that was impossible.
So in that brief moment as he walked by he whispered,
"Take courage. God knows." Unknown to Georgy, her
husband and 17 other members of the choir had also been
arrested that night. Nineteen of his friends, nineteen
brothers and sisters who would also spend the next years
of their lives in gulags and siblags, slaves of the
government. Most of them would never see their loved
ones again. *Arrests recorded in Moscow, and witnessed by heaven.*

Having never been in prison before, there was no
way Georgy could have anticipated what was going to
happen. For the next few days he would be kept in a cell
at the Lubyanka while waiting for his trial and sentencing.
Cells built for two were often forced to accommodate
eight. There were times when prisoners were actually
stacked on top of each other. But somehow they survived.
Those who were eventually released said that after the

Lubyanka prison, the gulag work-camp was a relief.

Days passed. He was not sure how many. Days of hardly being able to move. Days of being stripped of all human dignity. Days that some would not survive. But Georgy did. The words of the apostle Paul to the church in Corinth were a constant source of strength to him: *"We are hard pressed on every side, yet not crushed; we are perplexed, but not in despair; persecuted, but not forsaken; struck down but not destroyed—always carrying about in the body the dying of the Lord Jesus, that the life of Jesus also may be manifested in our body. For we who live are always being delivered to death for Jesus' sake, that the life of Jesus also may be manifested in our mortal flesh"*(2 Cor. 4:8-11).

The Bill of Indictment on Case N 653. Charged are:

Slesarev G. G.
Kolesnikov Ivan Matveyevich
Kondratyev Vas. Ivanovich
Lapshin Ilya Nikolayevich
Alferova Yekaterina Petrovna
Baranov Nikolai Petrovich
Shalier Y. G.
Shalier M. I.
Mend A. N.
Gornik B. P.

**Names of 9 others from the church
arrested with Georgy that night**

Interlude #4

YOUR HISTORY

Only a few were ever required to write an account of their past activities, and knowing that whatever they wrote would be used as evidence, not only against them, but against their family and friends, they wrote as little self-incriminating information as possible. This document would be placed in a permanent file at the Secret Police headquarters and could be used for anything deemed beneficial to the authorities. It could prove useful in future "purges."

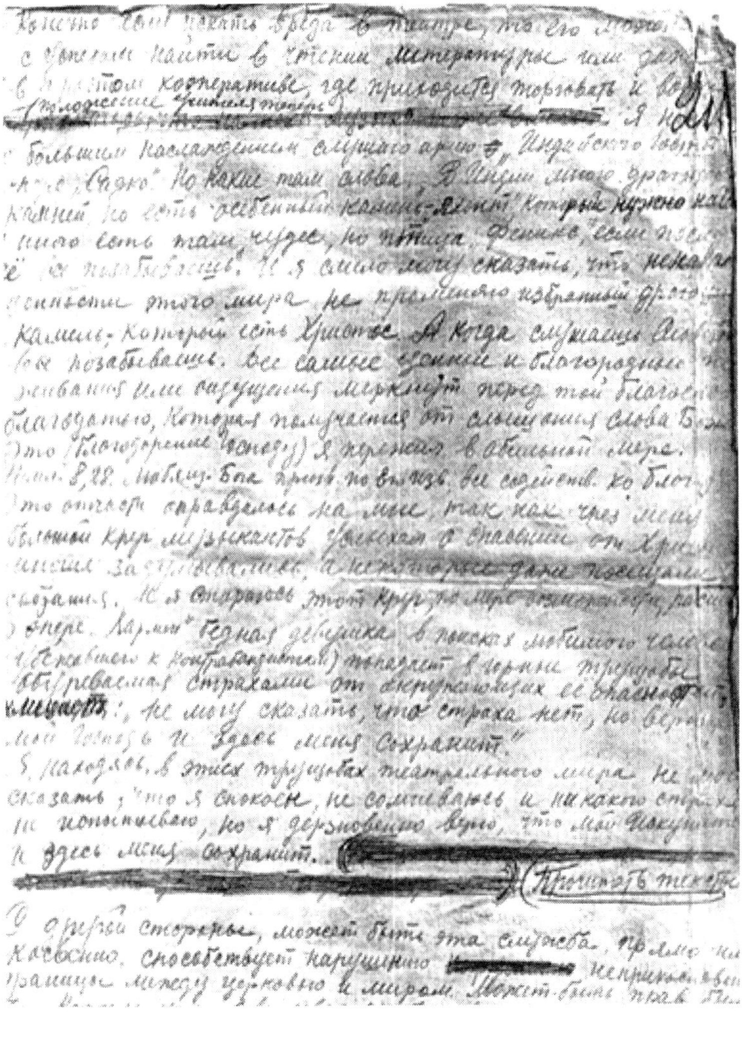

Photocopy of a page from Georgy's handwritten testimony

Five

MY STORY

He could not see the door being opened because he was at the very back of the cell, pressed up against the wall. All Georgy knew was that his name had been called. All but two of the other prisoners had to be moved into the corridor for him to get out.

They led him to a small room containing a table and chair. On the table were some sheets of paper and a pen. On the wall over the table was a picture of Stalin. The guard told him that he had been ordered to write down everything he could remember about his life. He had two hours to complete it. He heard the key turn in the lock.

"Why are they asking me to do this?" he wondered. "They have already decided that I am an enemy of the State. As far as they are concerned I am guilty. What purpose could they have in my writing down what has happened in my life? They are looking for something. What could it be? What are they going to use it for?" It was then he remembered a Scripture that said something about the enemy meaning it for evil but God meaning it for good. "This," he thought, "is an opportunity God is giving me to put my testimony in writing. I can enter a permanent *witness* into the Secret Police files, and God can use it in the life of anyone who reads it."

He then set about to write his story as though he was telling the world what God meant to him. He wrote about his childhood. He told the story of his father's coming to faith and the influence this had had on his own life. He recounted how God had used a Russian Orthodox monk to fan the flame in his heart for the things of God. Then he wrote about his years in Moscow. He wrote about how God brought him and Anna together and how they purposed to have a godly home. He recalled how his involvement in the Moscow church soon found expression in what he called "spiritual recitals."

"I formed an instrumental ensemble and was soon making a name for myself among Moscow Believers," he wrote. "This, however, led me to become increasingly concerned that my playing was generating more attention to my talent than it was directing people to God. I felt that the concerts in the church consisted more of showing myself off to the people than bringing glory to the One I was supposed to be representing. As far as I could tell, this was true of many of the other Christian musicians and singers. I felt that they were impressing the people, but they were not pointing them to Christ. They were using God and the church to display their talent. There was 'worldly' success, but no spiritual blessing.

"I remember the moment I began to think seriously about the call God had placed on my life. I began to prepare myself spiritually before I would perform, just as though it was a sermon I was going to preach. I saw that God wanted to use my violin playing itself as a *witness*. I soon discovered that people were turning to God while I was playing. Some were being converted even as I played my violin. The church leaders observed what was happening and told me to concentrate solely on my church work and give up playing 'in the world.' This greatly concerned me because I really felt that the Lord had given me my talent, not only to play in church, but to be a *witness* outside of the church.

"Not long after that I accepted an invitation to work at the Myack Theater where, with the help of God, I began talking a lot about Christ. I told the church leaders what I was doing but they didn't seem to understand. From there I took a job at the Kresha Restaurant on Tveriskaya street, and because of my *witness* I began to suffer some tough persecution, but still, I managed to lead one soul to the Savior.

"It was about that time that I began to realize how dependent I was on God for the courage and strength to take every step in my career. I remember the summer I became employed by the Forum Theater.[1] It was here that I began to face my greatest spiritual challenge. I decided to convert all who worked there. At first they put up with me, but then they launched a ferocious persecution against me. But still some were touched by the word of God and converted. The management began to threaten that they would banish me from Moscow if I did not stop *witnessing*. I was actually fired and rehired three times, but I did not complain, and received all the strength I needed from Christ. Every day I asked God to help me. I was issued a final warning by the Forum Theater management in which they referred to my 'preaching' at the theater, but I was assured by the Lord that it was not against me that they were doing this but against Him, and that He had a purpose in it all.

"The purpose God had in mind was beyond anything I could have imagined. I would soon be playing first violin in the Bolshoi Theater orchestra, a position that

---

1 The Forum Theater was, and still is, a landmark in Moscow. It is located near the Kremlin.

only God in His providence could have given me. I realized that because of my being faithful in *witnessing* for Him where I had been, He was now giving me a larger assignment. The last nine years at the Bolshoi have been the greatest of my career, not only because I have been able to play in such a wonderful orchestra, but because I have had so many opportunities to *witness* for my Lord. I spend[2] most intermissions in the theater lobby talking with people and looking for an opportunity to tell them about God.

"The most important thing to me in life is being a Christian. It is what guides everything I do. My first desire is to please God, in my family, in my church, and in my career. Because of what my Savior Jesus Christ has done for me I must tell others about Him."

Signed: *G. G. Slesarev*

---

2 Georgy uses the present tense here because it has been but days since his arrest, and he still sees himself as a member of the orchestra.

Interlude #5

A MARTYR'S (*WITNESS'S*) VIEW OF SUFFERING

Christians whose call to "persevere to the end" includes intense suffering, whether from persecution, illness, or some other hardship, are given clear instructions by God on what they are to do in order to remain faithful to the end. Interestingly, and not coincidently, these instructions are found in Scripture immediately following the list of those in the "roll-call of faith" who suffered so greatly for their *witness*.

Not only are we to take courage from their steadfastness, but we are to focus on the One for whom we are called to endure, our Lord Himself. Following the reminder that we are surrounded by "such a great cloud of witnesses," we are told to run the race *"looking unto Jesus, the author and finisher of our faith, who for the joy that was set before Him endured the cross, despising the shame, and has sat down at the right hand of the throne of God.* **For consider Him who endured such hostility from sinners against Himself, lest you become weary and discouraged in your souls.** *"* (Hebrews 12:2-30, emphasis added).

Unlike some "leaders" who are not themselves willing to pay the price they expect others to pay, our Leader set the supreme example and made the paramount sacrifice for His followers. Our Savior did not lead by decree, He led by example. It is this understanding of being a disciple of Christ that enables any "suffering follower" to not grow weary and lose heart.

Six

GUILTY!

There would be just a few more days in Lubyanka before being transferred to Butyrskaya, another Moscow prison, to await trial. Finally the day of the trial arrives. February 27. It has been five weeks.

"*Georgy Georgiyevich Slesarev; VINOVEN!!*[1] Guilty of *violating Criminal Code 58, Section 4. As an enemy of the State you are sentenced to five years of hard labor in the work-camp at Temir-Tau. Do you have anything to say?*" Anything to say? Of course he had something to say! He was innocent. He wasn't an enemy of the State. "I am Georgy Georgiyevich Slesarev" he thought. "I am a Christian. I am a violinist in the Bolshoi Theater orchestra. I am married and I have two small children. I love my country. I wouldn't do anything to hurt anyone." But he didn't say it. It would have been useless. No one ever said anything. The decision had been made. Nothing would change it. *VINOVEN!*

Then it was back to his cell to wait. Waiting for the unknown is the hardest waiting of all. Where was he going to be sent? North by northeast was where almost everyone went. Would he, by some miracle, get to see his dear Anna and the children before he was shipped away?

He tried to pray. It was so difficult to keep focused. The stench, the cold, the foul language. How could anyone do this to another human? But they were no longer

---

1 GUILTY!

human. He tried to talk to two of the prisoners who were pressed against him but it was impossible to carry on any meaningful conversation. How long could they last under these conditions? One prisoner did not. He collapsed and was removed.

Visitors? Had he heard correctly? The news spread rapidly from one cell to the next. Family members were going to be allowed to visit the prisoners! His heart began to race at the thought of seeing Anna and the children again. It seemed so long since the arrest, and though they were only 30 minutes away they might as well have been in another part of the world. He had not been allowed to have any communication with them. They had never been separated before. Now he would at least see them again. Oh, how he longed to hold them in his arms! But even seeing them would be more than he had dared hope.

The prisoners were herded into a holding room. Large pictures of Lenin and Stalin hung on two of the walls. One wall had the communist symbol of the hammer and sickle painted on it, and on the other wall were several viewing windows. Each window had a wooden shade with a guard assigned to lift and lower the shade at the beginning and end of the visitation time. With all the prisoners in the room, how was he going to be able to see his dear Anna and the children? "There are so few windows," he thought. He knew they would be there. He could hear voices on the other side of the wall.

Suddenly the shades were raised and the pushing and shoving began. The guards were trying to keep order. They seemed to be at least attempting to give everyone an opportunity to get to a window. Georgy got to one several times but could not see Anna. The men were shouting to their loved ones. Children were crying.

Anna and the children were having the same problem in getting to a window. "Where is Georgy? Where is he?" Suddenly Georgy heard little Mikhail's voice cry, "Papa!" Georgy turned to see the face of his little son pressed against the glass. He reached out to him just as the guard dropped the shade. Visitation was over. Georgy pled with him to raise it. "Please let me have just one moment with them. Please, please...." He could hear Mikhail on the other side of the window screaming, "Let me see Daddy! Let me see Daddy!" That would be the last time little Mikhail would ever see his father.

Interlude #6

THE TRAIN NO ONE WANTS TO RIDE

You never really knew where you were going. You certainly were not asked where you'd prefer to spend the next years of your life or how you would like to make the trip. You were a criminal who hadn't committed a crime. From the moment of your arrest you had no more rights. You hadn't surrendered them, there had been no fair debate—they were simply taken away. Your decision-making was now over, perhaps for the rest of your life. You had become a slave of the Party. If you complained, the screws were tightened even more, or you were annihilated. Your rank in society was that of an insect that could be stepped on at any moment.

The truth of this sinks in as you and hundreds of others are herded on to the train. Cattle would be treated better. You want to say something but your voice doesn't work. What would you say anyway? Conversation at this point seems to be the last thing you want to make. Everyone has the same look in their eyes—the helpless stare of resignation and fear.

The train begins to move. You are on your way to somewhere you don't want to go. The track on which the train is traveling was laid by other slaves whose rights were taken away. Though you have no way of knowing, this may be the one where so many died during its construction that at least one body is buried under every railroad tie, and there are thousands of kilometers of track across Siberia. And it takes an eternity to travel them.

Seven

SIBLAG AT TEMIR-TAU

"But wait." Georgy said to himself. "What am I doing thinking this way? I don't know where this train is going, but why do I have to? The One I trust the most knows. He's watching this train. He knows I am on it. I told Anna and the children that He would take care of us, and that includes me, right now. I said we had to trust Him. The worst they can do is harm my body, they can't harm my soul. The same God who put me in the Bolshoi Theater Orchestra is the same God who is allowing this to happen. It is not as enjoyable, but He is no less in charge. What my Lord went through for me was not enjoyable, so why should I complain? He put me where He did over these last years to be a *witness* for Him. He is sending me to wherever I am going to be a *witness* for Him there."

From this point on Georgy no longer questioned or feared. He saw this stage of his life as a part of God's plan. He discovered, as had other Christians before him, that God was faithful even in a communist work-camp. How could anyone survive year after year under such conditions without faith? Faith in God equals hope. The person who has no hope is to be most pitied. He is one who, because of circumstances, concludes that there is no reason to live. Few actually survived the work-camps who did not find something to hope in. If not, resentment and bitterness would pay its toll and they would eventually "lose it" and soon become another victim flushed down a gulag sewer.

Ironically, for the Christian, history has proven that in the most adverse of conditions the most beautiful flowers of God's grace have grown. And so it was with Georgy, as he began making the adjustment to this new chapter in his life.

His work-camp was located near the town of Temir-Tau, in Kazakstan, on the border of Siberia.[1] In this part of Russia the camps were called siblags rather than gulags. The difference ended there. Work-camp conditions varied little. You were a slave. You did as you were told. Any resistance could mean immediate extermination. You did not complain.

Oh, there were exceptions; there are always exceptions. There were those who did receive better than normal treatment. As in all Communist regimes informers played an integral part in keeping the lid on any uprising.[2] This was no less true in the work-camps. Those who volunteered to be "squealers" got more food, were assigned easier work, and were generally treated in a more humane manner. These were always eventually found out, however, but if the "squealer" knew in time that they had been found out, the authorities would provide a "safer haven." If not, they would be found lying in their bunks with their throats slashed.

Work-camps covered a large area of land. They

---

1 The actual description in the KGB files of where Georgy was imprisoned is as follows: "He served his prison term in the Akhpunsky division of the NKVD Siblag, or Siberian Camp, at the Temir-Tau mine."

2 On a visit to Czechoslovakia in the 1980's the author was told that as many as one out of every six citizens of that country was an informer. Whatever the percentage might have been in other counties, the practice was the same.

were themselves a small city, completely self-contained. Escape was next to impossible. The circumference looked like a maximum security prison. Guards, lights, fences, and barbed-wire. Oh, the barbed wire! What would Communism have done without barbed wire? And what if you did escape? Where would you go? Many of the gulags were located in remote areas where attempting to reach "civilization" on foot would mean certain death. So there you were.

Georgy (standing) with the Agitprop group

Georgy's first challenge came quite unexpectedly. When the work-camp Commandant discovered that such a fine musician had arrived, he advised him that he would play violin in an Agitprop entertainment group. These were groups who entertained with a political agenda. The music, the poetry, the skits, the comedy were all laced with communist propaganda. Though Georgy did not know what refusal to participate might mean, he initially felt that he could not be a part of it. But when the Commandant explained that he would be traveling to other areas of their work-camp "city" as well as to other siblags and gulags, he wondered whether this might not be a door God was opening to him. Knowing that there were other Believers in the work-camps he'd be visiting, he realized this could be an opportunity to offer help and encouragement. It would also extend the opportunities for sharing his faith. And so began a new ministry for Georgy Slesarev. He was now an "itinerant" siblag *witness*.

Interlude #7

GRACHOV FROM SAMAROV

It wasn't until the mid-fifties that the people of Russia and surrounding republics knew much of anything of what was happening behind the barbed wire of the work-camps. There were a few who were returned to their families, but that was the exception. Most, though initially sentenced for five to ten years, had their sentences renewed. An excuse to keep them imprisoned was easily fabricated, if fabrication was even needed. There was no one who would dare challenge those in authority.

At the Twentieth Party Congress in 1956, however, Nikita Khrushchev, then Party Boss, shocked the nation and the Party by denouncing Josef Stalin as a murderer, and he publically began to expose the atrocities that took place under the Stalin regime. But then, a short time later, frightened by what he had revealed and fearful that it could lead to his own demise, he began to back-track. He crushed the Hungarian uprising of 1956, then erected the Berlin Wall. Khrushchev was also responsible for sending his share of innocent citizens to the work-camps of Siberia.

Ironically, even while he was doing all this, he began the "repatriating" of many who had spent years in "slave-labor." These began to provide piece-meal information about what was going on behind the barbed-wire. It was not good news, nor was it wide spread information because the press were forced to maintain silence.

Among the few who were released prior to the Khrushchev period was a believer from Samarov named Yuri Grachov. Yuri had spent nearly 20 years in various work-camps, having his original sentence of five years renewed several times. He was in the work-camp at Temir-Tau when Georgy Slesarev arrived. He kept a diary of their relationship, carefully recording the meetings and conversations they had during the almost three years Georgy was imprisoned with him. On the twentieth anniversary of his arrest, Grachov was freed.

Some of the material in these following chapters is based on the record Yuri Grachov kept of his meetings with Georgy. Grachov called that period "The Grim Years of 1934-38."

Eight

THE AGITPROP CONCERT

Going to another Agitprop concert was the last thing Yuri Grachov wanted to do. During the years he had spent in work-camps he must have attended hundreds of them. He resented the using of art to promote the godlessness of communism. But he had no choice, he would go. As he had done so many times in the past, he would try to "tune out."

Yuri had heard this group before, but when the program began he noticed that there was a new member. There was something different about this young handsome violinist. Grachov was near enough to see his eyes. They were so dark. But unlike the other entertainers' eyes, they were alive. They were bright. And he played so beautifully! Could this be the noted Bolshoi Theater violinist he had heard had been arrested in Moscow? News had its own way of traveling through the work-camps.

When the concert ended Yuri did not speak to the young man, but he lingered long enough to make eye contact with him. He was not sure, he had to be careful...As he walked back to his post at the out-patient clinic, he prayed that God would somehow help him find out who this young man was.

"Are you Grachov?" he heard a voice behind him say, as he opened the door to the clinic. He turned, and there stood the violinist. "Yes," Yuri replied. "Then I need to talk to you," the young man said, as he turned and walked down the path that led to the back of the barracks. Grachov followed. The young man stopped and Grachov's heart began to beat with both excitement and fear. What would he say? The stranger smiled, and in that smile Grachov felt something that he had not felt, but had

longed for, for so long. "I am Georgy Slesarev, your brother," the stranger said, reaching out to embrace him. To feel the arms of someone who cared around him was more than Grachov could bear. As far as he knew, he was the only Christian in his part of the siblag. Tears began to stream down his cheeks. "How did you learn about me? I've had no contact with my family or any other Christians in so long," Yuri replied.

"I saw sister Shalier at Lubyanka in Moscow," said Georgy. "I began to pray that she and whoever else from the church who had been arrested that night would be sent to the same work-camp. I don't know where her husband is, but when I arrived at this siblag I discovered that God had arranged for several of us to be here. Though we ended up being scattered throughout the camp we were able to make brief contact when we first arrived and we prayed together that God would arrange things for His glory. Sister Shalier got a job in bookkeeping, which is her specialty, and I was asked to join this Agitprop troop. I hesitated for awhile, but when I realized that I would be visiting all the construction projects and all the sections of the prison camps, I thought that this would be a way of contacting other Believers and of being service to the Lord."

"The Lord Himself has sent you here," replied Grachov. "Not until you are isolated from any contact with other Christians for as long as I have do you realize how important Christian fellowship is. I have missed it so much. Only the sustaining power of the Spirit has kept me going. I had heard that a Bolshoi Theater violinist had been arrested, and there were rumors that he was a Christian. When I saw you at the concert tonight something in my heart reached out to you, and I thought that you must be that one."

"I have heard about you for years," said Georgy. "The brethren in Moscow have prayed fervently for you. There were rumors that you were in Temir-Tau, so when I realized I was coming here I was determined to find you. Soon after I arrived I was told that they had kept you here at this camp to work in the hospital, so I looked for you there but couldn't find you. Sister Shalier helped me check the lists and that is how I knew you were over in this area. I had been waiting for the night when we would perform in this part of the camp. I asked God to help me know who you were. I saw you watching me tonight, and I already felt the bond we have in our Lord. Only the blood of Christ can create what we feel. The affinity we have through our Lord makes us true relatives. We are real brothers."

Georgy went on to share with him as much news about the Believers in Moscow as he could. "The government is doing all it can to destroy the Baptist Union. There are many problems. There is talk that the authorities are going to close our building and force the church to move to a smaller place.[1] Many Believers are being spied on and arrested. Since Kirov's murder there has been an escalation of activity against Christians. It may not be long before Pavel Vasilyevich Pavlov, our pastor, is arrested.[2] Many tears are being shed all across our land by mothers, wives and children whose husbands, sons, and fathers are being sent off to these godless camps. Have you heard about our brother Yakov Wyzovsky? He has not been heard from in years. No one knows what has happened to him.

"I am sorry it has taken me so long to find you," Georgy continued. "I have wanted to meet you since I first heard you were here. The last word we had received in Moscow was that you had been sentenced to another five years and that they were moving you to another work-camp. How are you doing, my brother?"

"There is no real joy here," replied Grachov. "There has not been a single relative in the faith with whom I could feel at ease. Everyone suspects everyone. Dostoyevsky wrote that *what makes prison particularly*

---

1 The 2nd Baptist Church building was closed for most of 1935 and 1936. Many were arrested and what was left of the congregation moved to a smaller building.

2 Pavlov was soon to be arrested.

dreadful is that you are with a people of a totally alien spirit.' That's how I have felt."

"I understand," said Georgy. "We will talk more about this. But now I must go. They will soon be checking my dormitory, and it is almost a 30 minute walk from here. I will see if I can find an excuse for coming back to your area. Since my Agitprop duties exempt me from most of our squad's daily work assignments, I may be able to get permission to return, perhaps at a meal time. Let us pray that it will work out." They prayed, and the two brothers parted.

Interlude #8

THE PURGING WAVES

The arrests of Christian church members goes back to the days immediately following the 1917 Revolution. In January, 1918, Lenin announced a united effort to "purge" Russia of all kinds of harmful insects. Among these insects were church leaders: priests, pastors, nuns, monks, choir directors and choir members. In 1922 the newly named GPU (Secret Police) was called on to carry out a "church revolution" to remove the existing leadership and replace it with those who would have one ear turned toward heaven and the other toward the Lubyanka headquarters. The destruction of religious roots was the most important goal of the Secret Police, and this could only be accomplished by mass arrests of believers, especially leaders.

But the circle kept getting larger, and before long they were raking in ordinary believers by the thousands; old as well as young, and particularly women, who were considered to be the "most stubborn of all." Those convicted of "religious activity" were initially sentenced for from 5-10 years, and if they didn't die during that time, their sentences were almost always renewed. The general rule was that they would never be allowed to return to their families. Prostitutes, on the other hand, were given 3 years, with no sentence extension.

Yuri Grachov was part of the first wave, and by the time Slesarev arrived he had already spent 17 years as one of communism's insects. That he was ever released was a miracle. His handwritten memoirs, in five parts, were secretly passed from church to church, believer to believer, during the late 60's and early 70's. The last part of these memoirs told the story of his years with Georgy.

Nine

THE MESS HALL MEETING

The 5 am reveille was sounded by the beating of a hammer on a piece of a rail suspended near the staff headquarters. Georgy was already awake, so he was the first one to the bucket. It was another of those frigid mornings with the temperature somewhere around minus 30° Celsius, but the northerly wind coming out of Siberia made it seem much colder. Georgy, however, didn't notice the cold that morning. He was warm with anticipation of what was going to happen. He had received permission to visit Yuri's part of the camp, and he was excited. It had been several months since they had had their last talk, and so much had happened since then. He was anxious to share the news.

On each of the Agitprop tours Georgy had been able to make contact with other Believers, and always had an opportunity to share his faith. On one occasion he noticed a newly arrived inmate cross himself at a meal before dipping his spoon into the lukewarm broth. After the meal Georgy went to him and asked if he was a Believer. He became very nervous and unwilling to respond, but after a few minutes, as they were walking down the path past the prefabs, he confided in Georgy that though he had never been a Believer he had a mother who prayed for him. Since he arrived at the camp a few days before, he had been thinking about it. After several meetings the young man from the Ukraine had met his

57

Savior. God had heard the prayers of a devoted mother and had already placed a faithful *witness* in a communist work-camp to explain the way of salvation to her son.

Georgy was anxious to bring his friend up to date and to hear what had been happening in his life. Yuri was waiting at the Mess Hall. He had a hard time not showing how he really felt as he saw his brother in Christ approaching, but the two simply nodded to each other and got in line. Fortunately the line was not long and they only had to stand outside for a few minutes. Inside it would be warmer. After getting their bowls of stew they waited for a place that would seat the two of them. They watched as the prisoners ate the boiled black cabbage mush. In spite of the taste everyone ate slowly as though relishing every bite, but the truth of the matter was that mealtime was one of the few occasions that they felt they had at least some control over their lives. The eating part was strictly for whatever nourishment they might get out of the food in order to stay alive. It was not for enjoyment.

Their timing was good. As a space became available others were beginning to leave. This meant that they could have a private conversation without others listening in. They would have to hurry, though, because the lunch hour would soon be over.

"How are you, my friend?" asked Georgy. "I've been doing much better since we last met," replied Uri. "Just knowing that there is someone who knows where you are is a comfort. I know that our Lord is always aware of our situation, but you understand."

"My dear brother, I do understand," said Georgy. "I have had my moments, and if it were not for my conviction that God brought me to Temir-Tau to be His *witness,* I don't know how I would make it. I keep

58

reminding myself of our brother Paul the Apostle and what he said. I'm so thankful that I took the time to memorize as much Scripture as I did, though now that I don't have a Bible I wish I had learned much more. He said, *"Who shall separate us from the love of Christ? Shall tribulation, or distress, or persecution, or famine, or nakedness, or peril, or sword? As it is written: "For Your sake we are killed all day long; We are accounted as sheep for the slaughter." Yet in all these things we are more than conquerors through Him who loved us. For I am persuaded that neither death nor life, nor angels nor principalities nor powers, nor things present nor things to come, nor height nor depth, nor any other created thing, shall be able to separate us from the love of God which is in Christ Jesus our Lord."* (Romans 8:35-39).

"Oh, my brother Georgy, how I needed to hear that from you! I had a Bible and a few books, but they were stolen some time ago. I don't understand why anyone would do that. I have been like a man without food. I, too, am grateful for the Scripture I memorized, but how I miss my Bible! I wonder how many of our brothers and sisters in other parts of the world really realize the precious gift freedom is and how blessed they are to have a Bible. It is not until you are deprived of some things that you really appreciate their value."

"Dear Uri, my heart beats with yours. I have written a postcard to my Anna asking her to request permission to visit the city of Temir-Tau. I've asked her to bring me my Bible. I don't know whether she will receive my message, but I am trusting God to work it out. Now let me tell you very quickly what has been happening on my Agitprop tours." Georgy went on to tell him about the young Ukranian as well as the other opportunities for *witnessing* he had had, then he added, "Oh Yuri, I have wonderful news to share with you.

"In visiting one of the gulags last month, I met brother Mikhail Danilovich Timoshenko. He is now a grey-haired old man but is still full of faith in the lofty cause of reaching our land with the gospel. We have all heard about him and his perseverence for the Lord, but to get to meet him was a blessing beyond anything I could have expected. He is a wonderful man. He is steadfastly going after Christ. You remember that he was persecuted for his faith back during Czarist times, and he is still being haunted by the enemy. But it has left him undaunted. In the camp where he was about to complete another sentence, he led several souls to accept Christ so he has now been given another sentence for what they call 'seduction.' But his face still shines with the radiance of his Lord."

Yuri's own face lit up. "I have not only heard of him, but years ago I heard him speak. To me he has always been a hero of the faith. I am so thankful that he is still living and doing well. What an example such a life is for us! But how are our other brothers doing?"

"All are joyful," replied Georgy, "but most work on hard-labor teams. Some are very weak. Of course, each tries to support the other. They share parcels and bread, but still they are physically fading."

"And how many brothers and sisters are employed in constructing the Gorno-Shorskaya highway?" asked Yuri. Georgy threw up his hands. "There are so many of them that they cannot be counted."

"And how many brothers and sisters are in all the gulag and siblag camps?" Yuri asked. Closing his eyes for a moment and then bowing his head, Georgy replied,

"God is keeping the statistics. They are all in His Book of Life, inscribed in the blood of Christ. And God may be putting a special check mark by our brothers and sisters who are suffering so much for the gospel's sake. He knows all the exiles who lie in the unmarked graves of this land. He knows. That is all that counts."

"Friend," whispered Yuri. "We are being watched. We had better leave. May God grant us another opportunity to be together."

Interlude #9

SQUADS

There was a twofold motive behind the waves of arrests. One was to remove from society those whom the Party considered to be a threat, or who simply were considered to be undesirable for the future society they were working toward. The other reason was "free" labor. By creating the work-camps, they could exile the unwanted while putting them to work for the Party. This was seen as being much more productive than simply stepping on the "insects." Why not use them until they were of no more use, then step on them? The gulags and siblags were usually very large with many buildings or factories, each producing a different commodity for the government.

The work force within the camps was organized into squads. Each squad had a leader, and that leader was expected to meet or exceed a certain quota. This was a clever way of making sure everyone worked his knuckles to the bone because, if the squad did well, there was a little extra food for everyone in that squad. If the squad fell behind, however, the entire group would be penalized, not just in a cut-back of food but often with a tougher job assignment. So the prisoners egged each other on. If you were thought to be loafing, others would start shouting, "Who do you think you are? Do you expect us to go hungry because of you?" And so the days passed, and so the months turned into years, if you survived. Anyone who could not "produce" was considered to be eating food that another productive person could use. Anyone who was not fully in tune with the goal of the camp was occupying a bunk another more cooperative prisoner could use. And so the gulag flushing continued. It is believed that more were killed in the Communist gulags and siblags than all the fatalities of World War II. And this was being inflicted by a few, upon their very own people. During this period of history, Mother Russia lost 20 million of her children.

Ten

THE CLINIC MEETING

"I like spring," thought Grachov, as he worked on inventory in the quiet of the out-patient clinic. "In spring there are fewer health problems than in winter. In spite of still being in a work-camp everyone seems to be in better spirits. I don't have to deal with frozen feet and noses. Oh, the frozen feet! Sometimes they are so bad that amputation is required. But why bother doing that? It only saves a life for a few days. You are now useless to the camp and so you are flushed. I'll never get used to that. How I wish I were not here. I wonder what it is like on the outside? It has been so long I can't even remember. Oh well, at least they can't take spring away."

The squads were all at work. No one had bothered him for several hours, when suddenly the door opened. As Grachov turned to see who it was, he was greeted with a hearty *"Zdravstvuy, moy dorogoy brut!"*[1]

"Georgy Georgiyevich Slesarev!" Yuri cried, stepping around the counter to embrace his friend. "What are you doing here? I have wondered where you were. It seems that the time between our meetings gets longer. But thank God you are still alive and you have come to visit me. That's all that counts at the moment. I am doing fine. And you, my dear friend?"

---

1 "Hello, my dear brother!"

"In God's strength I keep going on," Georgy replied. "We must trust Him every day."

"What is the word about our brothers and sisters? Have you seen any of them?"

"Yes, I have been with some of them. Since our last meeting, however, several of them have died and one brother just disappeared. It is suspected that he was executed. Some of those who have been in the camps for several years are rapidly weakening. My heart goes out to the women. Why do they put women on those hard-labor jobs? I have wished I could take the place of one of them, but that is not possible. I take comfort every day that they will soon be rewarded. I also thank God that I can still *witness* for Him, though I am meeting with more and more hostility. But my job is to plant the seed and that is what I must keep doing. God has me here for that, and to be an encouragement to the brethren. Now tell me, Yuri, how are you doing? Last time, when we met in the mess hall I did all the talking. I have regretted not hearing more from you. Please tell me what has been happening with you, my dear brother? I'm afraid that I have only a few minutes. I slipped away on my own, but I just had to see you. I prayed that we would find a quiet place to briefly talk, and the Lord has answered my prayer."

"God has been testing me, Georgy, and for some time I was not passing His test. You remember I told you that my Bible and books had been stolen? Well, I was becoming bitter over that. I even found myself not wanting to help anyone with medicine in order to pay them back. I kept thinking of how much I had done for many of them. How often I was up in the night trying to keep them well so they would not be annihilated. There is one from Tallin who I have especially suspected to be the thief. He is always saying cutting remarks to me and to others about my being a crazy Christian. I have wanted to refuse to give him any help. But then one day I remembered our Lord. He cured and saved people, and what did they do to Him? They spit on Him, they beat Him and they crucified Him. And then I remembered what His response was when they did all that. He said, 'Father, forgive them, for they do not know what they are doing.' It made me feel so terrible about my attitude. I asked God to forgive me and help me to look at my enemies through the eyes of Christ. My aversion for these people disappeared, I am glad to say. I began to feel sorry for them because they are going to perish in hell."

"God has already given you the victory," Georgy said, as he clenched both Yuri's shoulders in his hands. "We must be on guard at all times, dear friend, because the devil wants to destroy our testimony. Let me tell you, I have also had my struggles in this area, but thank God, He has also given me victory. When I think of what this savage barbaric government has done to the Church in Russia, I have found it very difficult to look at them as Christ looks at them. I have been more like Jonah, wanting them to perish. Does our Lord still love those who have confiscated our Bibles and books of faith? Yes. Does our Lord love those who destroyed all the irreplaceable material collected over the years on the history of our brotherhood by brother Ivanov-Klyshnikov? Yes, He does. Does our Lord love those who have destroyed so many of our beautiful church buildings, along with the magnificent oil paintings of Biblical scenes done by some of Russia's leading artists? Yes, He does. Does our Lord love those who have stolen hundreds of thousands of fathers and mothers from their children, planning never to give them back? Yes, He does.

"It is true that they are vested with power. That's what the Scriptures say. Even they are God's servants, but like God did with the pharaohs, He may be hardening their hearts in order to prove His glory. We may not live to see it, Yuri Grachov, but the day will come when the people of God will be delivered, and the glory of God will fill our land. As Christ was crucified and buried, so must we, His body, be crucified and buried. Right now our brotherhood is being destroyed and buried, dear Yuri, but take hope, the day of resurrection will come and the gates of hell will not be able to stand against the Church of our Lord. There will be a day of resurrection. Let us pray that we all will stay faithful to the end."

"Yes," replied Uri, "let us pray that we will remain faithful to the end."

"Now, my friend, I must be going," said Georgy. "They will soon be looking for me. God has given us this quiet time together to meet as brothers in a foreign land. But before I leave I have exciting news to tell you. Do you remember that I had sent a message to my dear Anna, asking her to request permission to bring me a Bible? She received my postcard and has sent a message that she will be arriving soon in Temir-Tau, with my Bible. Yuri, oh Yuri my friend, God is still on His throne. We will have a Bible soon."

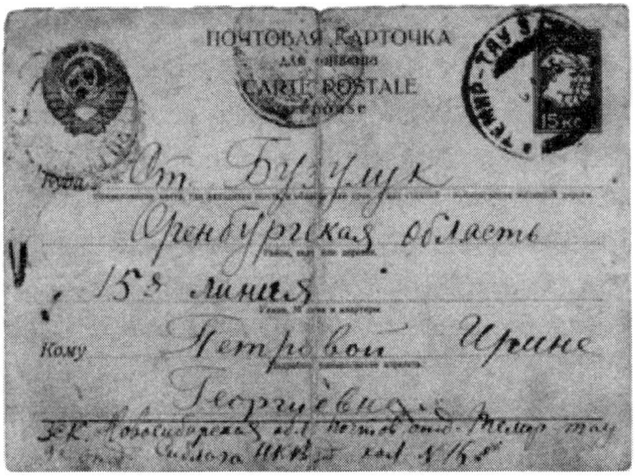

ПОЧТОВАЯ КАРТОЧКА

CARTE POSTALE

Куда ст. Бузулук

Оренбургская область

15-я линия

Кому Петровой Ирине

Георгиевне

З.К. Новосибирская обл. почтов. отд. Темир-тау

[illegible] Сиблага НКВД [illegible] № 165

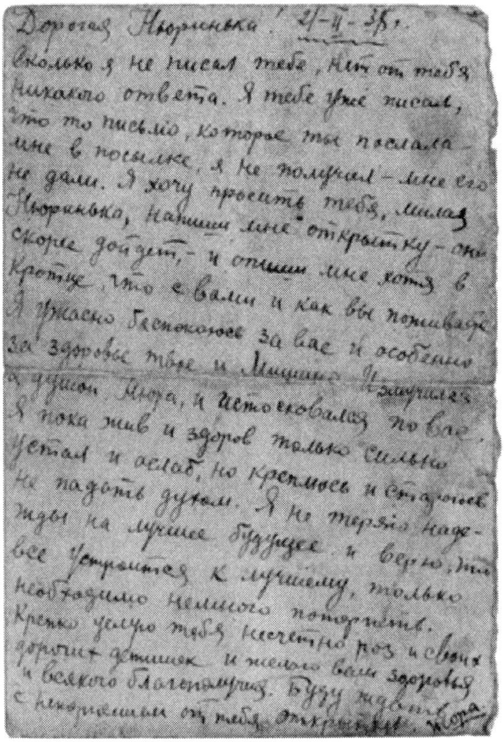

Дорогая Нюронька! 21-II-38 г.

Сколько я не писал тебе, нет от тебя никакого ответа. Я тебе уже писал, что то письмо, которое ты послала мне в посылке, я не получил — мне его не дали. Я хочу просить тебя, милая Нюронька, напиши мне открытку — она скорее дойдет, — и опиши мне хотя в кратце, что с вами и как вы поживаете. Я ужасно беспокоюсь за вас и особенно за здоровье твое и Мишино. [illegible] Мора, и истосковался по вас. Я пока жив и здоров только сильно устал и ослаб, но крепюсь и стараюсь не падать духом. Я не теряю надежды на лучшее будущее и верю, что все устроится к лучшему, только необходимо немного потерпеть. Крепко целую тебя несчетно раз и своих дорогих детишек и желаю вам здоровья и всякого благополучия. Буду ждать с нетерпением от тебя открытку. Жора

Picture of a postcard Georgy sent to Anna

Interlude #10

THE BIBLE

Georgy's relationship with the work-camp commandant had been quite cordial, perhaps because he enjoyed hearing Georgy play the violin. At times it even seemed as though he went out of his way to accommodate him. Georgy, however, had never asked for any favors— that is, until now. When he received the first note from Anna that she had received permission to make the trip, he knew God was working on their behalf. Then, when the word came about her arrival time, and that little Anna was also coming with her to Temir-Tau, he knew that a miracle was in the making. Now all he needed was permission to meet them in town, or to have them visit the camp. He knew that visiting the camp was probably out of the question, so he began praying that God would grant him favor in the eyes of the commandant when he went to request a pass.

The commandant not only granted him permission, but told Georgy that he had a pleasant surprise for him. He told him he would have the surprise ready when he came to pick up the pass. Georgy had no idea what it might be, and he didn't spend any time thinking about it because his thoughts were all focused on seeing his beloved wife and little daughter again. He could not believe it. He would be seeing them in three days, and he would again have his Bible.

Eleven

THE TEST

He couldn't sleep; but then, he didn't really try. He lay there reliving the memories of past years. How smitten he had been the first time he saw Anna at church! She was the most beautiful sight he had ever seen. How nervous he was the evening he had proposed! They had laughed about it later. Then there were the letters he had written to her about his ideas on marriage, and the long talks they had together, dreaming of children and a godly home. These and countless other scenes played across the screen of his mind. The hours sped by as he thought of how God had blessed them, first with little Anna, then a few years later with Mikhail. He heard again the squealing of the children as the family went by horse and sleigh to the bath house. He recalled the walks in the park, and Sundays at church. Happy tears were flowing freely as he turned over in his bunk to kneel, just as He had done many times before in the middle of the night, to pray for his family and others. "Oh God, You have been so good to me. Forgive me for ever complaining. You have met my every need, and now, You are going to let me see my two Annas again."

The commandant was waiting for him. He greeted Georgy with a handshake, which Georgy thought to be a bit out of the ordinary. He was told to be seated. His being in that office was unusual, considering the fact that he was a prisoner. The office was not large. There were only two chairs—the one he was seated in, and the one behind the desk. The walls were bare, except for the customary pictures of Lenin and Stalin, and a picture of the Commandant with some high-ranking official with rows of ribbons and medals on his chest. The desk was small and old. One leg was missing, and the corner was propped up with bricks and books. On the desk was a picture of two small children. The picture was angled just enough for him to see it. There was also a small trophy of a hockey player, a loose-leaf notebook, and lots of papers. Georgy wondered how much of the Commandant's life was captured in just those few things. He wanted to talk to him about God. He had prayed for him many times and had always felt that this was not an assignment the Commandant relished having, but one that he had to fulfill before the next promotion.

The Commandant was sitting behind his desk reading something on a sheet of paper. Georgy wondered whether he should speak, perhaps he could start by thanking him for the permission to meet with his wife and daughter. He could then tell him how thrilled he was that he was going to have his Bible again, and how important it was in his life. But before he could say anything the Commandant stood up, and still studying the sheet of paper said: "I have been able to make a special arrangement for you. I have received permission to offer you your release from the Temir-Tau Siblag. I have arranged for you to be reunited with your family and to resume your career. You may take your belongings with you into Temir-Tau. You, your wife and daughter will be put on a train to Moscow this evening. You will be given your tickets and visa at the train station. I am very glad for you."

Georgy couldn't believe what he was hearing. How could this be? He had completed less than three years of his five-year sentence. They never did this. Was this a dream? Of course God could do anything He chose to do for His children, but....

"Before you go, however," the Commandant continued, "I need you to sign this paper. Please read it carefully. What you do with it will determine your future." He handed the sheet of paper to Georgy.

Georgy's hands had always been steady. A violinist of his stature had to have steady hands. But now as he held the paper they began to shake uncontrollably. He was even having difficulty seeing the words on the paper. "What does it mean? In just a few minutes I will be free again. I will be able to go home. I will be with my dear Annas and little Mikhail. I will be back with my brothers and sisters at the church. He said I could resume my career." The words on the sheet of paper began to come into focus:

> *By my signature below, I, G. G. Slesarev agree to cease from talking to anyone about God. I will never again attend a church meeting. I will never again associate with Christians, either in public or private.*
>
> *In return, the State will provide me and my family the usual care and protection afforded to all faithful citizens of this great land of Russia.*
>
> *To affirm my compliance with this document I agree to report weekly to the Ministry of Security of the Russian Federation, located in the GPU headquarters, Lubyanka Square, Moscow.*

Georgy Georgiyevich Slesarev

Witnessed by:

Date:_____

Georgy was stunned! His first impulse was to scream, NO! NO! As all the emotions of his Kubansky-Cossack heritage whelmed up inside of him he thought he would explode. But he didn't. Instead, he suddenly began to weep. The Commandant had seen his share of crying before, but Georgy's was different. It made him feel very uncomfortable, and he left the office. Georgy was alone. Alone with the most wrenching decision he had ever faced. He began to understand what they were doing. They knew that by letting him be with his Annas again, they could break down his resistance. They knew that this would be the way to get him to sign a document that would not only silence his *witness* in the future, but would destroy his past.

He tried to read the paper again, but he couldn't see through the tears. Overwhelmed, he dropped to his knees. He had nowhere else to go but to God. Words he had sent heavenward in the apartment over two years before when Anna had cried, "But what are we going to do without you?," again rose from the deepest recesses of his being.

"Boze pomogy! Boze pomogy!"[1]

"God, it doesn't ask me to renounce my faith in You. It just says I won't be able to join my brothers and sisters in fellowship and worship. I could worship You with Anna and the children. It doesn't ask me to say I don't believe in You. It just says that I won't be able to talk about You. I won't be able to tell anyone about how much You care for them. I won't be able to *witness*. I won't be able to *witness*. I won't be able to *witness*. Oh, God! I won't be able to *witness*!

"But God, that is what I live for, to tell people about You. What is a Christian without witnessing? I don't know how I could live without letting someone know about your love. I would die. If I never again told anyone about You, I would be denying You. Wouldn't I be denying You? I can't do that. I can't do that. But God, Anna and the children need me, and I need them. You know how much I long to be with them. You are the only One who knows how much I miss them. You know how my heart has pained."

He could not think any more. There were nothing but sobs. But in the midst of the sobs the battle between his flesh and his spirit was being fought. In the midst of the sobs, the final step in the *witness's* denial of himself was being made. He would choose to keep taking up his cross. He would keep following his Lord.

In Vladykaskaz he put his hand to the plough. He could not let it go in Temir-Tau.

As he rose from the floor, he was suddenly flooded with the peace that passes all understanding. When the

---

1 "God help! God help!"

Commandant returned a few minutes later, he saw a poised 34-year-old young man who had just been "freed." Georgy stood and handed the tear-soaked, unsigned sheet of paper to the Commandant, who didn't seem surprised to find it unsigned. Georgy knew he would not be allowed to meet with his Annas now, but he ventured to ask the question anyway. "May I see them just one last time?" To his surprise, his request was granted. He would be escorted into town within the hour.

Interlude #11

BETTER ALIVE THAN DEAD?

There are numerous accounts of Christians who were offered their freedom in exchange for a denial of their faith in God; most refused, however, and were subsequently annihilated. But there were a few who did recant, not realizing that, more often than not, there was no intention on the part of the authorities to release them. They would subsequently be exterminated and the document would then be used to discourage and weaken other Believers in the camps, as well as to undermine the Church back home.

The question has been asked, Would Georgy have been similarly treated if he had failed to pass the test? Would they have actually allowed him to return to society as they had promised in the document? No one really knows. However, in the opinion of some who lived through those days, the Slesarev case was unique in that he was a Believer with a higher than normal profile in the world due to his work in the theater world. He was a Christian who was well-known for his unashamed *witness*.

Some years later, when "little Anna" became involved in the Moscow music scene, she asked musicians who had worked with her father what they remembered of him. She found that they would always begin by talking about his great musicianship, but then, without exception, they would tell her what a very special man her father was. They would express their feelings in such terms as, "He was a very good man. He was different from anyone else. He was not just a good musician..." One, interestingly, called him an "angel."

In light of this, returning him to the people who knew his passion for witnessing as one who was silent and unwilling to talk about his Lord, would have been more beneficial to the State than having him annihilated. He would have lived the life of a traitor.

Twelve

DA SVIDANYA, MY LOVE![1]

Anna Gorlova was singing in the alto section of the church choir the Sunday morning Georgy had visited the Second Baptist Church of Moscow. Now as the Temir-Tau Siblag gate shut behind him he recalled the moment he first saw her. "She is the most beautiful creature I have ever laid eyes on," he remembered thinking. But as he got to know her, it was her inner beauty that really captured his heart.

Anna had been reared in the Moscow area by devoted Christian parents. A friendship grew into a more serious relationship, and soon they became aware that the Lord intended for them to marry. Georgy began writing letters to Anna, letters laying down guidelines upon which he felt their marriage needed to be based, guidelines that with God's help would insure their having a Christ-honoring home in the midst of an atheistic society. Anna was as committed to having this kind of home as was Georgy. She had kept all his letters, or as she had once teasingly called them, "Georgy's sermons," in a small box, as a reminder of their commitment. Little had they known the role those letters would play in his arrest.

Now, as he and his "escort" approached the town, the emotions of the last several hours merged with the anticipation of seeing his Annas again, and he thought his

---

1 "Goodbye, my love!"

heart was going to burst. He wondered how he could tell them of the decision he had just made. It might be more than they could bear. "Oh God, help me be strong for their sake," he prayed. "Help me to know what to do."

Then, there she was, his Anna. The recent years had taken their toll. He would never know what she had been through—the harassment, the shunning by neighbors, the fear of being removed from the apartment and relocated to another part of the country, the abuse "little Anna" and Mikhail had to endure at school, all the things that were now a part of their lives. Her eyes looked so tired, but to Georgy, they were more beautiful than he had ever seen them. He realized how brief were the ten plus years they had had together, and how long the last two and one-half years had been.

They embraced. He held and held the two of them in his arms. He picked "little Anna" up. She had grown so much. How he wished Mikhail could have come. The meeting was brief. The escort must have been told to stay within ear-shot. Anna had brought a parcel for him— some food, a spoon, a pair of boots, socks, and a few other pieces of clothing. And of course, she had brought his Bible. Tears filled Georgy's eyes as he held it for the first time in over two years. There would be more tears. They would all cry. Anna would whisper news of what was happening back in Moscow. She would tell him how they were doing. She would report on what was happening at the church, the arrests that were continually being made, and how the church had been forced to move to a smaller meeting place. She would tell him that Vasile Pavlov, their pastor, had gone into hiding. The GPU would soon find him.

But Anna would not know of the decision Georgy had made. He realized that he could not tell her yet. Several months later she would get a card. The card would tell it all. It would tell her what had happened. It would ask her to please understand. He knew she would. The card would say that he had cried all the way back to the camp, and all night long. It would say how much he loved her and the children, and how he thought his heart was going to explode. It would also remind her that their hope and strength was in God, and that He was going to always provide for them.

The "escort" announced it was time to leave. "Why do we have to go so soon?" Georgy asked. "Can we have just a few more minutes?"

"Two more," was the reply. Two more minutes. The last two minutes they would ever have together. What do you do? What do you say? As Georgy held them in his arms he prayed. "*Gaspody, You said You would never leave us or forsake us. We cling to that promise. Please take care of them. Please take care of them.*"

Da Svidanya, my love....

Interlude #12

AN ETERNAL PERSPECTIVE

There is a remarkable contrast between the western church's view of suffering for the Gospel's sake and that of the rest of the world. Whereas the western Christian generally sees suffering as something to be avoided, almost at any cost, and the "victorious Christian life" as one of ease, many other parts of the Christian world see "suffering for Christ's sake" as a part of life. Inherent in the call to follow is the willingness to die.

When my wife Patricia and I first began ministering in the Soviet Union in 1985, this contrast was underlined for us in a personal way. We discovered in conversations with those who had spent years in prison that generally they saw their imprisonment as an assignment from the Lord. We never heard any complaints. In fact, there was a general reluctance to even talk about the sacrifices they had made. It seemed as though those years were seen as a part of their walk with their Lord and thus, an opportunity to be light in the darkness of that world. There were exceptions, of course, but those were not encountered.

Another contrast that illustrates the difference in perspective that many in the West have is seen in the way we pray when faced with hardship. In the Book of Acts, the praying of the persecuted church was not for release or relief from suffering, but rather for the strength and grace to endure and overcome in the midst of it. And part of that grace was the strength to pass the ultimate test, the choosing against all that our humanity is begging and longing for—the ultimate choice against the flesh. Yet how often we think first and only of escape.

Thirteen

THEY CANNOT STOP THE MUSIC

"Dorogoi droog, ya tuck rud tiebya videt. Kuck pozivaiesh?[1] It has been such a long time. Why have you not come? I had tried to inquire about you but could get no word." So it was that Yuri greeted Georgy.

"What has happened? How were you able to come here?"asked Georgy.

"Oh, my dear friend," said Yuri. "You have not heard? I have been given my release. In just a short while they will be escorting me out of this place I have been forced to call home for so many years. For months now I have been waiting for some word. And when I received it, I was afraid I would not see you again. I requested permission to talk with you before I left."

"I have been barred from the Agitprop team and have been transferred to a general works squad," Georgy replied. "It all happened very quickly four months ago. I could not get word to you. I had received permission to see Anna, but before I was to leave, the Commandant asked me to come to his office. He said he had a surprise for me. Oh Yuri, they asked me to deny my Lord. In exchange for my freedom, they asked me to sign a paper that I would never talk about Him again."

"They asked you to deny your faith?" said Yuri.

_____

1 Dear friend, I am so glad to see you. How are you doing?"

"No, not to deny that I believed in God, but that I would never tell anybody about Him again." Georgy's voice broke, and Uri heard a sob that came from the deepest recesses of his friend's soul. *"Ya ni mog sdelat eta. Ya ni mod sdelat eta."*[2]

"For these last four months I have been laboring in the Temir-Tau iron-ore mine. Look at my hands." Yuri looked at his friend's hands. Hands that had once so tenderly held the bow and violin; hands that had once played so skillfully before the most sophisticated audiences in the world; hands that God had used to create music that led souls into His kingdom were now unrecognizable. The fingers were broken, bruised and scarred. One finger was swollen to twice its size. There were no nails left on the others.

"You are now unable to play the violin," said Yuri, tears filling his eyes. His heart ached for his friend. Music had been so much of his life. It was a language that Georgy could speak like few ever could. Now, though not yet 35 years of age, he would speak it no more.

"Yes, my brother, I am dead to the art now. I will never play again. I do not recognize these fingers. They don't seem to belong to me. I now drill gruesome rock cliffs and break stone, but my dear brother, don't grieve. Christ has become so close to me. He is closer than He has ever been. My flesh is weak, my body is tired, but this is just a temporary moment in the time of eternity that is soon to open up to me. They have stopped me from playing the violin, but my dear, dear friend, you know, you

---

2 "I could not do it. I could not do it."

understand, that *they cannot stop the music that plays inside my heart."*

"It grieves me to see you the way you are, dear brother. To see your body so weak and your face so drawn and thin," said Yuri.

"Oh, but you must be happy with me," Georgy encouraged. "Our Lord told His disciples, *'Blessed are those who are persecuted for righteousness' sake, for theirs is the kingdom of heaven'*" (Matt. 5:10).

"Yes," said Yuri. "We must be happy." The two brothers prayed together, and with that, embraced. *"Proshay, proshay, dokole svidemsya."* [3]

A year later, Yuri returned to Temir-Tau. He returned to find out what had happened to his friend. He was told that he was no longer there, that he had been taken away from the central section of convicts and assigned to work on the building of the Gorno-Shorskaya highway. Yuri kept looking. He went to the road building site, but couldn't find his friend. He went from place to place, from work squad to work squad, but Georgy was not to be found. In his memoirs he writes: *"Some are driven away in train cars, with thick bars on the windows. Many rest in graves, with mounds as the only reminder that they ever lived. I look at those mounds in the taiga,*[4] *I do not know under which one my friend might be lying. The mounds have tested my faith...and I have*

---

3 "Farewell, farewell, until we meet again." "Proshay" is sometimes used as a farewell in Russian when it is very unlikely that the parties will ever see each other again. That would be true for Georgy and Yuri, here on earth.

4 A Russian, moist, sub-arctic forest of spruce and fir-like trees that begins where the tundra ends.

seen the newly burned belongings of those who were shot..."

And so it was with Georgy Georgiyevich Slesarev, *witness*. The official files of The Ministry of Security of the Russian Federation, Novosibirsk, read:

> *On February 28, 1938, Slesarev G. G. was charged with taking part in a counterrevolutionary organization and carrying out anti-Soviet propaganda among convicts [witnessing]. On March 12, 1938, by the verdict of the UNKVD troika of the Novosibirsk region, in keeping with articles 58-2,8, 9, 10, 11, he was convicted and sentenced to execution by shooting. The sentence was carried out on March 17, 1938.*

In 1989, in addition to the material found in the KGB files, Georgy's daughter Anna and son Mikhail sought further clarification of their father's death and burial. A letter received from Ministry of Security, City of Kemerovo, in October, 1992 included the following:

> *Because of law violations during those years, the archive case omits the place where G. G. Slesarev was executed and buried. We have sent a note to the Tashtagol of the Kemorovo region which will send you G. G. Slesarev's death certificate.*

> *By decision N. 370 of June 1956, the Siberian Military District Tribunal exonerated Slesarev G. G. because he committed no crime. You can get an exoneration document by writing to the Siberian Military District Tribunal and citing number and date. The address to write to is: 630012, Novosibirsk, st. Gogol 8.*

POSTLUDE

Anna and "little Anna" boarded the train that evening not knowing whether or not they would ever see Georgy again. Their own future was uncertain. Within weeks after their return, however, they found out. They would have to leave Moscow. Because Anna was listed as the wife of an "enemy of the State," they were taken to the city of Buzuluk, near Oranburg, in the Ural Mountains. Buzuluk was an area where many of the relatives of convicted "criminals" were sent to live. They were not officially imprisoned, but it was here that they were "detained." They were not allowed to return to Moscow nor do any traveling outside the city. Each week Anna and the children were required to sign in at the headquarters of the GPU.

It was during this time that she received three postcards from Georgy dated January 24, February 2, and March 1, 1938.

Unknown to Anna, the day before Georgy had written the last card he had been charged with counter-revolutionary (*witnessing*) activity. On March 12 he was sentenced to die by firing squad. Five days later, the sentence was carried out. He never mailed the card. As they came to escort him to his execution, however, the card was one of several personal items he grabbed to take with him. But as they were leading him across the snow, the card slipped from his grasp. Another prisoner, watching what was happening, saw the card fall and retrieved it. He eventually was able to mail it to Anna. It read:

The Commission has notified me that I will soon be able to leave here and choose where I want to live. I of course am going to ask permission to move to Buzuluk where you and the children are. I am so tired. I am having trouble believing what I hear. I kiss you and the children. Be strong! Pray that we will soon be back together. With love in my heart. Georgy

Four years later, in 1942, Anna was given permission to move to within 100 kilometers of Moscow, to the city of Alexandrov. "Little Anna" was returned to Moscow to further her music studies. She was given a room on Sretinka street near her grandmother, just around the corner from the Lubyanka. (Her grandfather had died of pneumonia in Tashkent in 1930). Now that Anna's visa categorized her as the wife of an enemy of the State, she was not permitted to work as a school teacher, for which she had trained. She found a job as a waitress in the Alexandrov train station restaurant where she worked for the remainder of World War II. There she became acquainted with many people, including several members of the police force who helped arrange for "little Anna" to visit her. On one occasion she was also able to visit her daughter in Moscow.

Anna eventually was permitted to move back to Moscow where she died in June, 1985, at the age of 82. She was buried next to her mother in the town of Himke, a northwest suburb of Moscow. Mikhail, the son, worked for many years for the city of Moscow where, as Director of Clock Maintenance, he oversaw the upkeep of all the City's public clocks. He is now seventy-one.

After she was returned to Moscow when her mother moved to Alexandrov, "little Anna," already advanced in her music studies, decided to train as a nurse so she could help her country during World War II. She worked as a surgeon's assistant in a military hospital, and recalls that period as being "very difficult years." After the War she continued her studies, becoming one of Moscow's finest mezzo-sopranos, majoring in Verdi, Tchaikovsky, and Bizet operas. After years on the stage, she began a career of teaching voice. She presently teaches voice at Moscow's School for Advanced Actors, within 200 meters of the Bolshoi Theater, as well as at the Logos Christian Music Academy in Moscow, where my wife and I also teach on occasion. Anna Georgiyeva Davydova has been a priceless source of information. Without her, this story could not have been told.

"little Anna" with the author, Ron Owens

"AND THERE WERE OTHERS..."

By faith Abel...was commended...By faith Enoch ...By faith Abraham was enabled...By faith Isaac... Jacob... Moses...By faith the people passed through the Red Sea...By faith the walls of Jericho fell...By faith Rahab... And what more can we say...about Gideon, Barak, Samson, Jephthah, David, Samuel, and the prophets who through faith conquered kingdoms....

And then there were others...who "were tortured, not accepting deliverance that they might obtain a better resurrection. Still others had trial of mockings and scourgings, yes, and of chains and imprisonment. They were stoned, they were sawn in two, were tempted, were slain with the sword. They wandered about in sheepskins and goatskins, being destitute, afflicted, tormented–of whom the world was not worthy. They wandered in deserts and mountains, in dens and caves of the earth. *And all these, having obtained a good testimony through faith, did not receive the promise, God having provided something better for us, that they should not be made perfect apart from us"* (selected verses from Hebrews 11).

These "others," though heirs to the promise of God, did not live to see the promise fulfilled because God planned "something better for us," in giving us who follow them a part in their being perfected. The fulfillment of the promise to them is waiting on us.

But that is not all. In the very next verse the writer to the Hebrews cautions us that even as these "others" wait to be perfected through what we do, they are watching *us*. *"Therefore we also, since we are surrounded by so great a cloud of witnesses,* let *us* lay aside every weight, and the sin which so easily ensnares us, and let *us* run with endurance the race that is set before *us*, looking unto Jesus, the author and finisher of our faith, who for the joy set before him endured the cross, despising the shame, and has sat down at the right hand of the throne of God" (Hebrews 12:1-2, emphasis added).

Need any more be said than what the writer to the Hebrews has said? All the "Slesarevs" who have preceded us; all the men, women, boys, and girls who have laid down their lives for Christ and the sake of the Gospel are watching what we, who follow them, are doing with the same priceless treasure that they considered worth dying for.

The music that the most severe persecution and torture could not extinguish has been passed on to us. How well are we playing it?

THE MUSIC PLAYS ON

The witness of Georgy Slesarev in the Moscow music and arts world did not end with his arrest and death. Others have faithfully carried the torch over the years, and today, opportunities never before dreamed of are open to Christians to witness in this segment of Russian society that so greatly needs the light of the gospel.

The profits from the sale of this book will assist in the establishing of a Christian Center For The Arts in Moscow. This Center will house the Logos Choir and Orchestra, a group of professional Christian musicians under the direction of Evgeny Goncharenko that has been functioning since 1991; the Academy of Church Music, already in operation for 20 years; the Logos Children's Choir and other ministries. A piece of property has been offered for the building of the Center. It is located in the town of Himke, where Anna, Georgy's wife, is buried.

For information about this ongoing ministry please use the contact information below.

RON & PATRICIA OWENS
P.O. Box 5444
Bella Vista, Arkansas 72714
Tel: 479-855-7136
Email: Ronowens3@aol.com
Web site: www.owensministries.org